My Beloved
A Love Letter

Jeannette Luby

© 2022

Unless otherwise indicated, all Scriptures are taken from the *King James Version*.

Scripture quotations marked (NLT) are taken from the Holy Bible, New Living

Translation, Copyright © 1996, 2004, 2015 by Tyndale House Foundation. Used

By permission of Tyndale House Publisher, Inc., Carol Stream, Illinois 60188.

All rights reserved.

Scripture quotations marked (NKJV) are taken from the New King James Version®.

Copyright © 1982 by Thomas Nelson. Used by permission. All rights reserved.

Scripture quotations marked (AMPC) are taken from the Amplified Bible, Copyright ©

1954, 1958, 1962, 1964, 1987 by The Lockman Foundation. Used by permission.

Take note that the name satan and related names are not capitalized. I chose not to acknowledge him, even to the point of violating grammatical rules.

Dedication

To my Beloved Jesus—Yeshua
The King of my life—the Lover of my Soul.

A heartfelt thank you to Pastor Cathie Hightshoe for your invaluable help in editing
and
To Pastor Sara Vidulich for your creativity in designing the
beautiful cover of this book.
I dearly love you, both!

My Beloved
A Love Letter

Contents

Introduction 1

My Beloved 3

Dear Reader— 15

Dear Heavenly Father— 17

Endnotes 19

My Beloved
A Love Letter
By Jeannette Luby

Introduction

Recently, as I was worshipping in the Spirit at church—one of our anointed worship leaders began leading us in a beautiful worship song of adoration of Yeshua—Jesus.

Dawn Ledesma, so wonderfully follows the LORD's leading—bringing us into the Glorious Presence of G-d—as she flows with the Holy Spirit.

The lyrics in this song speak about how beautiful He is—*He is*—the *Most Beautiful.*

As I sang—and I worshipped—standing in the back of the sanctuary—

Yeshua said to me, "*You*—are *My* Beloved."

"*You* are the most beautiful—*to Me.*"

I stood still—perfectly still—soaking in—and saturated in the sweetness of His Words.

But—He was saying that to—all of us there—worshipping our King.

This book—is what He said—and how He feels about me—*and*—how He feels and what He thinks about—*you!*

His heart longs for a deep, intimate relationship with *you*—so He can tell you—how much He loves—*you!*

Maybe you have never heard about His Love for you before—

Or—maybe you just need to be reminded—as we all do.

I pray you will believe—and receive what He says—*to you*.

I pray that you will soak in His beautiful and glorious promises to you.

Let Him enrapture your heart with His Precious words—that they would be as honey on your lips.

This is His Love Letter—*to you—His Beloved*.

My Beloved

You—are My Beloved.[1]
I Love you—with an Everlasting Love.[2]
My Love will last forever—I will never stop Loving you.[3]
I chose you—long before I made the earth—the sky—the oceans.[4]
I chose you before I formed you—in your mother's womb.[5]
That is how much I Love you.

I am jealous over you. You are My Beloved.[6]
I will not share you with any other—you are precious to Me.[7]
I have chosen you—I have set you apart.[8]
I have made you pure and blameless.
I have made you—holy—My Beloved one.[9]
You are Royalty—you are holy—I have brought you out of the darkness—into My Kingdom of Light.[10]

I will never leave you—not ever.

I will not abandon you—not ever.[11]

I have great compassion, grace, and mercy for you.[12]
You can trust in Me—I Am Faithful to you.[13]

I Am Trustworthy. I will *never* betray your love.[14]

I will protect you—and cover you—in the shadow of My wings.[15]
As a wedding chuppah—I cover you.[16]
My Truth surrounds you—like a Shield.[17]

You can rely on Me to be Truthful with you—*always*
Because—I Am the Truth.[18]
I will never lie to you—not ever.[19]

I Love you.

Every day—every hour—every minute—every second.[20]

You are on My Mind.

I do not stop thinking about you.
And—all My thoughts for you—are full of peace and *all* good things.
To give you a future—and a hope![21]

Because you—My Beloved—are My treasured possession.[22]
I have so, so many good, good gifts for you.

And—I will *not* change my mind—you do not have to wonder—
Or worry—[23]
That someday I will change My Mind. I will not.[24]
For My Covenant with you—is *forever*—for *eternity*.[25]

I delight in you.[26]

You are a Crown of Beauty in My Hand—you are a Royal Diadem.[27]

I will quiet all your worries, troubles, and fear—with My Love.

My Beloved: A Love Letter

You bring so much joy to Me—that —I sing My Song—of Love—over you.[28]

I desire to spend time with you—and
I want you—to come close to Me.

Do not be hesitant to ask me for what you want—
I *want* to give you the desires of your heart.[29]
You will lack for nothing.[30]
Know this—My Beloved—when you look for Me—you will find Me.[31]

Because—

I Love you.

I never sleep—I watch over you day and night.[32]

No matter where you go—[33]
Or what you are doing—whether you are coming—or going[34]
I Am—Watching over you.[35]

Furthermore—I have assigned My Holy Messengers—My Deputies—
To be as a thorny hedge of protection around you—[36]
As you walk along the path of your Destiny.[37]

My Love for you is so great—that it exceeds any fixed number or amount—
It is greater—than *any measure* on the earth.[38]
So great is My Love for you—I *joyfully lavish* it upon you.[39]

I surround you—*with My Love.*
And—your hope is *in Me*.[40]

I Love you so much—that I have called you—My Glorious and Rich inheritance—abundant and beyond value.[41]

I Love you so much—that I placed My Kingly Seal—My Royal Imprint upon you—so that all would know—*you*—belong to Me[42].

The Seal I placed upon and in you—is not ordinary—not what some might think—

No—this Seal is not made of wax—or even molten gold—or liquid silver.

The Seal I placed upon *you*—the mark I placed upon *you*—is Holy Spirit.

He is the Authentication—should anyone question you—or should *you* doubt.
He is the Guarantee of the inheritance that I have set aside for you.
He *is* the Proof—that I chose you—and that *you belong to Me.*[43]
He also is the Pledge—*My* Pledge—*My* Covenant—*to you.*[44]

I Love you.

It pleased Me and—it was by *My will* that I chose you. [45]
I have chosen you—to be a part of Me—to be a part of My Kingdom—
To be a part of My family![46]

I Am your Good Shepherd—[47]

And—you—*My Beloved*—are my little ewe lamb.[48]

6

My Beloved: A Love Letter

I Am not merely a hired hand—who doesn't care for you—[49]
A hired hand would not save you—as I have!
A hired hand would run away when he sees a wolf coming after you![50]

But I—Am your Shepherd—the One Who laid down His Own Life—to save you![51]

I Am your place of quiet Rest—and Peace.
I Am like a refreshing bubbling brook to your soul.[52]

I Love you.

My Beloved—
I rescued you—I redeemed you—
I called you by name—
I gave My Life—for you—for you are Mine.[53]

I Love you.

I engraved you—yes—I literally carved you—into My Hands.[54]

In doing so—I made a Promise—A Covenant.[55]

That—I Am yours—and you are Mine.[56]

I know about all your aimless wanderings—[57]
So—*Beloved*—hide *My Precious Words to you—in your heart.*[58]

They will keep you from sinning.

I know *each* tear that you have cried—
I have kept them—all—in a bottle.
And I keep a record of them all—in My Book. [59]

I will give back to you—all the parts of your soul—
That the enemy has stolen.[60]
And where he has caused you trauma and pain—[61]
I will heal every part of your heart[62] and mind.[63]
I Am—your Healer.[64]

Don't be afraid or discouraged—
I will give you all the strength you need.[65]
I Am your Strength—[66]
And I hold you up in My Right Hand.[67]

And—if you hold My Hand—I will lead you in the Way of Righteousness—[68]
I will lead you on a straight path.[69]
I will send Goodness and Mercy to follow you—*always.*
And—you—My Love—will live in My House—*forever!*[70]
Because—

I Love you.

I don't think you really know.
If you did—
You wouldn't think about yourself the way—
That you sometimes do.[71]

If you really—*knew.*

Know this—I don't look at your outward appearance—[72]
It matters not to Me—
Nor am I impressed with fancy clothes or hair—
I don't even look at those things![73]

You—are always the most beautiful to Me![74]

For I have clothed you in the garments of *My* Salvation[75]

My Beloved: A Love Letter

I have given you—*My* Robe of Righteousness.[76]

I have given you My Scepter—which represents—My Divine Authority.[77]

And—you have My Staff—which is My Protection and Support—along the way—even when all *seems* bleak.[78]

They will bring you comfort.

All these wonderful things are yours—because—My Beloved—

I Love you.

My Father rescued you—from the kingdom of darkness—and He placed you into *My* Glorious Kingdom—the Kingdom of Light.[79]
Because I redeemed you with My very Life—with My Blood.
Because of that—My Father has forgiven all your sins—all of them.[80]
Though your sins *were* like scarlet—I washed them and cleansed them—
And—now they are as white as the *pure snow!*[81]

They—are covered by My Blood.[82]

My Beloved—your sins are in the deepest sea—*forever.*[83]

They are as far as the east is from the west—*forever!*[84]

I remember them—no more![85]

I have redeemed your life from destruction![86]
I have encircled you with My favor and tender Love—Like a Beautiful Crown—My Beloved.[87]

9

I am telling you these things—so you will know—how *great*—how *deep*—*my love is for you.*[88]

I know all the things—you have ever felt.[89]
Every pain—and every trauma—
For I felt them—Myself—for you.[90]

My Beloved—I know how it is to be betrayed by one you trust.
I know this—because I was betrayed by one who was dear to me.
I was betrayed—by a kiss.[91]

My Beloved—I promise—I will *never* ever—do that to you.[92]

I Love you.

I Am—the Alpha and the Omega.[93]
I Am—the Beginning and the End.[94]

I Am—the King of Kings and Lord of Lords.[95]
I Am—the Lion of the Tribe of Judah.[96]

I became—the Lamb of G-d—[97]
I became—the Sacrifice for sin.[98]
I completely erased—wiped away all that would have been required of you.
All the legal requirements against you—were nailed to My Cross.
They were nailed *onto Me!*[99]

I carried every sin—from your past—from your present—and from your future—on My body.

My Beloved: A Love Letter

By doing this—I disarmed and defeated the enemy—and made a public spectacle of him.

It was a Triumph—My Beloved!!!

For all to see—what I did for you![100]

It was a celebration of Victory and Freedom!

For you—for the one I Love.

Now—I Am sitting—at the Right Hand of My Father—
Far above all principalities—powers—and dominions
And above every name that is named—in Heaven and on earth.[101]

And My Father—has qualified you to sit there—with Me.[102]

He has made you—part of Me—of My Own Body.[103]

And know this—My Beloved
The fullness of all I have—is *in you*—as well—for *you are part of Me*
And—*I am Part of you.*[104]

Now—
I am—waiting—
Waiting for the day when I will come for you—[105]

I Am waiting for the day the Father says—'It's time!'[106]

And—then—finally I will come to you—and you will be with Me—
Forever.[107]

That is how much *I Love you*—My Beloved.

But—while *I* am waiting—
While—*you*—are waiting for—*Me*
I want you to know—

I Am preparing a Glorious and Wondrous Place for you.[108]

I can hardly wait for you to see it.[109]

When you come to live with me forever—
I will wipe away *every tear* from your eyes.[110]

We will have a Wedding Feast—the Wedding Feast of the Lamb.[111]

You—*My Beloved*—My Bride—will have prepared yourself—in fine white linen—pure—and unblemished.[112]

O—My Beloved—

We will *celebrate!*[113]

There has never been a celebration like there will be—when you are finally with Me.[114]

As you wait for Me—
Don't become discouraged.[115]

Remember this—*My Beloved*—
Nothing can separate you—from My Love.

Nothing.[116]

Always look for Me—[117]

I promise I will return for you[118]
and until I do—remember

I Love you.

My Beloved: A Love Letter

Since I cannot be with you right now.
You have the Holy Spirit with you—Whom My Father sent to you—
To Comfort you—[119]
To give you Wisdom[120]
To guide you in all Truth—[121]
And—He reveals the Mysteries of My Kingdom.[122]

O—My Beloved—

I want you to so look forward to Me coming back for you—[123]

I Love you.

Your Worth—to Me—*is so great*—[124]
I gave My Life for you—you are My Love.[125]

As you wait—

I will give you—rest
And—I will carry all your heavy burdens.[126]

Come to Me—in our secret place of intimacy—[127]
And I will give you Living Water.
For *I Am*—the Living Water—and if you drink from Me—
You *will never* be thirsty again.[128]
Come—drink from My Well—the Fountain of Life[129]
From which flows—Rivers of Living Water.
And—if you drink from My Well—Rivers of Living Water will flow out of your heart.[130]
It will overflow and water the seed around you—making it ready for My Harvest.[131]

I want you to desire Me more than anything—more than anyone—
As I desire you.[132]

I Love you.

You are worth more—than *anything* on this earth to Me.

You—are My Beloved.

You—are My Bride.[133]

O, say to Me—My Beloved—

"*My Beloved is mine and I am His.*"[134]

Rise up—My Beloved—My fair one—and come away with Me.
For—the winter is past—the rain is over—and gone.

The flowers appear on the earth—
The time of singing has come!
Rise up—My Beloved—My fair one—and come away with Me.[135]

Set *Me*—as a Seal upon *your heart,*
As a Seal upon your arm—
For—many waters cannot quench the Love I have for you—[136]

My Beloved.

Come away—with Me............

Dear Reader—

Perhaps you have never heard about the extravagant Love that G-d has for you—before reading this book. Just as the Love Letter says—Jesus—

G-d's Only Son came to this earth to pay the greatest price for my sin and—for your sin. He died on the cross willingly—so that you and I could be in Heaven with Him someday. And—He *wants to have a relationship with you*—now—

He wants *you*—to be *His Beloved*.

Or maybe—you *have* heard this before—but never received Jesus into your heart and life—and you are not yet part of G-d's Family.

Jesus has all those things He spoke about in the letter—for *you*.

All those promises are in His Word—the Bible.

He has a wonderful plan—a Destiny for your life. He wants to have a sweet, intimate relationship with—*you*—and He desires that you walk in the freedom and victory that *He* paid the ransom for. He wants to heal every pain and trauma that you have had in your life. He wants to heal every place in your broken heart.

If you have never received Him into your heart—but would like to do that today—I invite you to pray this prayer with me. Please—pray it out loud—speak the words *from your heart*—not just your mind—or intellect. Just as Jesus' Love Letter was from *His Heart to you*—speak to Him—*from your heart.*

Jesus is saying this to you, dear one—

> *"Behold, I stand at the door and knock. If anyone hears My Voice and opens the door, I will come into him and dine with him, and he with Me."*
>
> *Revelation 3:20 NKJV*

He is standing at the door of your heart—I pray that this is the day that *you invite Him in*—that *you* would truly be—*His Beloved.*

Dear Heavenly Father—

Forgive me of *all* my sin. Jesus—come into my heart. Wash me and cleanse me. Set me free. I receive Your forgiveness and Your gift of salvation and eternal life. I believe that You died for me and that You rose again.

I ask that you fill me with Your Holy Spirit. Thank You, that You have made me a New Creation—and that I no longer live in condemnation and guilt and shame. I thank You that You remember my sin—*no more*! I thank You, LORD that *You* now live in me. I ask that You give me deeper revelation of Your Love for me and the Destiny You have for me. Thank You, Jesus—that You are coming back for me someday! I thank You that I will someday live in Heaven with You forever. Thank You, Jesus—that *I am— Your Beloved—and You are mine! You belong to me—and I belong to You!*

In Your Name,
Amen."

You are *His Beloved* and you have all the benefits and privileges of being a child of the King of Kings! You have been translated into the Kingdom of Heaven! And—*all* the blessings He has for you—*are yours*!!!

> "The Spirit Himself bears witness with our spirit that we are children of G-d; and if children, then heirs—heirs of G-d and joint heirs with Christ."
>
> **Romans 8:16, 17a NKJV**

> "But as many as received Him, to them He gave the right to become children of G-d, to those who believe in His Name."
>
> **John 1:12 NKJV**

G-d Bless You—dear one!

Endnotes

1   [Song of Solomon 1:16- "Behold, thou art fair, My beloved." KJV]

2   [Jeremiah 31:3- "Yes, I have loved you with an everlasting love; Therefore, with lovingkindness I have drawn you." NKJV]

3   [I Chronicles 16:34- "Give thanks to the LORD, for He is good! His faithful Love endures forever." NLT]

4   [Ephesians 1:4- "just as He chose us in Him before the foundation of the world," NKJV]

5   [Jeremiah 1:5- "Before I formed you in the womb, I knew you;" NKJV]

6   [Exodus 34:14- "(for you shall worship no other god. For the LORD, Whose Name is Jealous, is a jealous G-d)," NKJV; II Corinthians 11:2- "For I am jealous for you with godly jealousy. For I have betrothed you to one husband, that I may present you as a chaste virgin to Christ." NKJV]

7   [Isaiah 43:4- "Since you were precious in My Sight, You have been honored, And I have loved you;" NKJV;

8   [II Corinthians 6:17- "Come out from among them and be separate, says the LORD. Do not touch what is unclean, and I will receive you." NKJV]

9   [I Thessalonians 5:23- "Now may the G-d of peace make you holy in every way and may your whole spirit and soul and body be kept blameless until our LORD Jesus Christ comes again." NLT]

10 [I Peter 2:9- "You are a chosen generation, a Royal priesthood, a Holy nation, His Own special people, that you may proclaim the praises of Him Who called you out of darkness into His Marvelous Light;" NKJV]

11 [Hebrews 13:5a- "I will never leave you." NKJV; Hebrews 13:5b- "I will never abandon you." NLT]

12 [Psalms 86:15- "But You, O LORD, are a G-d full of compassion, and gracious, Longsuffering and abundant in mercy and truth." NKJV]

13 [Lamentations 3:22, 23- "Through the LORD's mercies we are not consumed, because His compassions fail not. They are new every morning; Great is Your Faithfulness." NKJV]

14 [Psalms 89:33,34- "My lovingkindness I will not utterly take from him, nor allow My faithfulness to fail My covenant I will not break, nor alter the Word that has gone out of My lips." NKJV; Psalms 118:8- "It is better to trust in the LORD than to put confidence in man." KJV]

15 [Psalms 91:1- "He who dwells in the Secret Place of the Most High shall abide under the shadow of the Almighty." NKJV]

16 [Psalms 19:5- "Which is like a bridegroom coming out of His chamber," NKJV; Joel 2:16- "Let the bridegroom go out from His chamber, and the bride from her dressing room." NKJV]

17 [Psalms 91;4- "He will cover you with His Feathers. He will shelter you with His wings. His Faithful promises are your armor and protection." NLT]

18 [John 14:6- "Jesus saith unto him, 'I Am the Way, the Truth, and the Life." KJV]

19 [Numbers 23:19- "G-d is not a man, so He does not lie. He is not human, so He does not change His mind. Has He ever spoken and failed to act? Has He ever promised and not carried it through?" NLT.

20 [Psalms 139:17, 18- "How precious also are Your thoughts to me, O G-d! How great is the sum of them! If I should count them, they would be more in number than the sand;" NKJV]

21 [Jeremiah 29:11- "For I know the thoughts that I think toward you, says the LORD, thoughts of peace and not of evil, to give you a future and a hope." NKJV]

22 [Deuteronomy 14:2- "You have been set apart as holy to the LORD your G-d, and He has chosen you from all the nations of the earth to be His own special treasure." NLT]

23 [I Peter 5:7- "Casting the whole of your care (all your anxieties, all your worries, all your concerns, once and for all) on Him, for He cares for you affectionately and cares about you watchfully." AMPC]

24 [James 1:17- "Every good gift and every perfect gift is from above, and comes down from the Father of Lights, with Whom there is no variation or shadow of turning." NKJV]

25 [Hebrews 9:15- "He is the Mediator of the New Covenant, by means of death, for the redemption of the transgressions under the first covenant, that those who are called may receive the promise of the eternal inheritance."]

26 [Psalms 18:19- "He delivered me because He delighted in me." NKJV]

27 [Isaiah 62:3- "You shall also be a crown of Glory in the hand of the LORD, and a Royal Diadem in the hand of your G-d."]

28 [Zephaniah 3:17- "The LORD your G-d in your midst, the Mighty One, will save; He will rejoice over you with gladness, He will quiet you with His Love, He will rejoice over you with singing." NKJV]

29 [Psalms 37:4- "Take delight in the LORD, and He will give you your heart's desires." NLT]

30 [Psalms 23:1- "The LORD is my Shepherd; I shall not want." KJV]

31 [Matthew 7:7- "Ask, and it will be given to you; seek, and you will find; knock, and it will be opened to you." NKJV]

My Beloved: A Love Letter

32   [Psalms 121:3- "He Who keeps you will not slumber." NKJV]

33   [Psalms 32:8- "I will guide you along the best pathway for your life. I will advise you and watch over you." NLT]

34   [Psalms 121:8- "The LORD keeps watch over you as you come and go, both now and forever." NLT]

35   [Psalms 33:18- "Behold, the eye of the LORD is on those who fear Him—On those who hope in His mercy," NKJV]

36   Psalms 34:7- "The angel of the LORD encamps all around those who fear Him and delivers them." NKJV]

37   [Psalms 91:11, 12- "For He shall give His angels charge over you, to keep you in all your ways. In their hands they shall bear you up, lest you dash your foot against a stone." NKJV]

38   [Ephesians 3:17-19- "being rooted and grounded in love, may be able to comprehend with all the saints what is the width and length and depth and height— to know the love of Christ which passes knowledge; that you may be filled with all the fullness of G-d." NKJV]

39   [I John 3:1- "Behold, what manner of love the Father has bestowed on us, that we should be called children of G-d!" NKJV]

40   [Psalms 33:22- "Let Your unfailing Love surround us, LORD< for our hope is in You Alone." NLT]

41 [Ephesians 1:18- "I pray that your hearts will be flooded with Light so that you can understand the confident hope He has given to those He called—His holy people who are His rich and glorious inheritance." NLT]

42 [Ephesians 1:13- "In Him you also trusted, after you heard the Word of Truth, the Gospel of your Salvation; in Whom also, having believed, you were sealed with the Holy Spirit of Promise," NKJV]

43 [Ephesians 1:14- "Who is the Guarantee of our inheritance until the redemption of the purchased possession, to the praise of His Glory." NKJV]

44 [Hebrews 10:15-17- "But the Holy Spirit also witnesses to us; for after He had said before, 'This is the covenant that I will make with them after those days, says the LORD: I will put My laws into their hearts, and in their minds, I will write them,' then He adds, 'Their sins and their lawless deeds I will remember no more.'" NKJV]

45 [Ephesians 1:5- "For He foreordained us (destined us, planned in love for us) to be adopted (revealed) as His Own children through Jesus Christ, in accordance with the purpose of His will (because it pleased Him and was His kind intent." AMPC]

46 [John 1:12, 13- "But to as many as did receive and welcome Him, He gave the authority (power, privilege, right) to become the children of G-d, that is, to those who believe in (adhere to, trust in, and rely on) His Name—who owe their birth neither o bloods

My Beloved: A Love Letter

nor to the will of the flesh (that of physical impulse) nor to the will of man (that of a natural father), but to G-d. (They are born of G-d!) AMPC]

47 [John 10:11a- "I Am the Good Shepherd." NKJV]

48 [II Samuel 12:3- "But the poor man had nothing, except one little ewe lamb which he had bought and nourished; and it grew up together with him and with his children. It ate of his own food and drank from his own cup and lay in his bosom; and it was like a daughter to him." NKJV]

49 [John 10:11b- "The Good Shepherd gives His Life for the sheep." NKJV]

50 [John 10:12- "A hired hand will run when he sees a wolf coming. He will abandon the sheep because they don't belong to him, and he isn't their shepherd. And so, the wolf attacks them and scatters the flock." NLT]

51 [John 10:15- "As the Father knows Me, even so I know the Father; and I lay down My Life for the sheep." NKJV]

52 [Psalms 23:2- "He maketh me to lie down in green pastures; H leadeth me beside the still waters." KJV]

53 [Isaiah 43:1- "'Fear not, for I have redeemed you; I have called you by your name; you are Mine.'" NKJV]

54 [Isaiah 49:16- "See, I have inscribed you on the palms of My Hands; Your walls are continually before Me." NKJV]

55 [Genesis 3:15- "He shall bruise your head, and you shall bruise His Heel." NKJV; Isaiah 7:14- "Isaiah 7:14- "Therefore the LORD Himself shall give you a sign; behold, a virgin shall conceive, and bear a son, and shall call His Name Immanuel." KJV]

56 [Song of Solomon 2:16- "My Beloved is mine, and I am His." NKJV]

57 [Psalms 119:10- "I have tried hard to find You—don't let me wander from Your commands." NLT]

58 [Psalms 119:11- "I have hidden Your Word in my heart, that I might not sin against you." NLT]

59 [Psalms 56:8- "You number my wanderings; You put my tears into Your bottle; are they not in Your Book?" NKJV]

60 [I Peter 5:8- "Be sober, be vigilant; because your adversary the devil walks about like a roaring lion, seeking whom he may devour." NKJV]

61 [Psalms 23:3a- "He refreshes and restores my life (myself)." AMPC]

62 [Isaiah 61:1b- "He has sent Me to Heal the broken-hearted," NKJV]

63 [I Corinthians 2:16b- "But we have the mind of Christ." KJV; Psalms 30:2- "O LORD my G-d, I cried out to You, and You healed me." NKJV]

64 [III John 1:2- "Beloved, I pray that you may prosper in all things and be in health, just as your soul prospers." NKJV]

65 [Isaiah 41:10a- "Fear not, for I am with you; be not dismayed, for I am your G-d. I will strengthen you, Yes, I will help you," NKJV]

66 [Psalms 27:1- "The LORD is my Light and My Salvation; whom shall I fear? The LORD is the Strength of my life; of whom shall I be afraid?" NKJV]

67 [Isaiah 41:10b- "I will uphold you with My Righteous right hand." NKJV]

68 [Psalms 23:3b- "He leads me in the paths of righteousness (uprightness and right standing with Him—not for my earning it, but) for His Name's sake." AMPC]

69 [Psalms 5:8- "Lead me, O LORD< in Your Righteousness because of my enemies; make Your Way straight before me." NKJV]

70 [Psalms 23:6- "Surely Goodness and Mercy shall follow me all the days of my life, and I shall dwell in the House of the LORD my whole life long." NKJV]

71 [Galatians 4:7, 9- "Now you are no longer a slave but G-d's own child. And since you are His child, G-d has made you His heir. So now that you know G-d (or should I say, now that G-d knows you), why do you want to go back again and becomes slaves once more to the weak and useless spiritual principles of this world?" NLT; II Corinthians 5:17- "Therefore, if anyone is in Christ, he is a new creation; old things have passed away; behold, all things have become new." NKJV; Romans 8:1- "There is therefore now no

condemnation to those who are in Christ Jesus, who do not walk according to the flesh, but according to the Spirit." NKJV; John 1:12- "But as many as receive Him, to them He gave the right to become children of G-d, to those who believe in His Name." NKJV]

72 [Proverbs 31:30- "Charm is deceitful, and beauty is passing, but a woman who fears the LORD, she shall be praised." NKJV]

73 [I Samuel 16:7- "For the LORD does not see as man sees; for man looks at the outward appearance, but the LORD looks at the heart." NKJV]

74 [Ephesians 2:10a- "For we are G-d's Masterpiece." NLT]

75 [Isaiah 61:10a- "For He has clothed me with the garments of salvation," NKJV]

76 [Isaiah 61:10b- "He has covered me with the robe of righteousness." NKJV]

77 [Psalms 23:4- "Your rod and Your staff, they comfort me." NKJV]

78 [Psalms 23:4- "Your rod and Your staff, they comfort me." NKJV]

79 [Ephesians 2:6- "and raised us up together and made us sit together in the Heavenly places in Christ Jesus." NKJV; Philippians 3:20- "For our citizenship is in Heaven, from which we also eagerly wait for the Savior, the LORD Jesus Christ." NKJV; Colossians 1:13- "For He has rescued us from the kingdom of darkness and transferred us into the Kingdom of His Dear Son," NLT]

80 [Colossians 1:14- "in Whom we have redemption through His blood, the forgiveness of sins." NKJV]

81 [Isaiah 1:18- "Though your sins are like scarlet, they shall be as white as snow; thought they are red like crimson, they shall be as wool." NKJV; Psalms 51:7- "Purge me with hyssop, and I shall be clean; wash me, and I shall be whiter than snow." NKJV]]

82 [I John 2:2- "He Himself is the sacrifice that atones for our sins—and not only our sins but the sins of all the world." NLT]

83 [Micah 7:19- "He will again have compassion on us and will subdue our iniquities. You will cast all our sins into the depths of the sea." NKJV]

84 [Psalms 103:12- "As far as the east is from the west, so far has He removed our transgressions from us." NKJV]

85 Hebrews 8:12- "For I will be merciful to their unrighteousness, and their sins and their lawless deeds I will remember no more." NKJV]

86 [Psalms 103:4a- "Who redeems your life from destruction," NKJV]

87 [Psalms 103:4- "and crowns me with love and tender mercies." NLT]

88 [Ephesians 3:18- "And may you have the power to understand, as all G-d's people should, how wide, how long, how high and how deep His love is." NLT]

89 [Hebrews 4:15- "For we do not have a High Priest Who cannot sympathize without weaknesses, but was in all points tempted as we are, yet without sin." NKJV; Matthew 4:1-3- "Then Jesus was led up by the Spirit into the wilderness to be tempted by the devil. And when He had fasted forty days and forty nights, afterward He was hungry. Now the tempter came to Him, he said, 'If You are the Son of G-d, command that these stones become bread.'" NKJV]

90 [Isaiah 53:4- "Surely, He has borne our griefs and carried our sorrows; yet we esteemed Him stricken, smitten by G-d and afflicted. "NKJV]

91 [Matthew 26:49- "Immediately he went up to Jesus and said, 'Greeting, Rabbi!' and kissed Him." NKJV]

92 [Psalms 89:33- "But I will never stop loving him nor fail to keep My promise to him." NLT; II Timothy 1:12- "for I know Whom I have believed and am persuaded that He is able to keep what I have committed to Him until that Day." NKJV]

93 [Revelation 1:8- "I Am the Alpha and the Omega, the Beginning, and the End, says the LORD G-d, He Who Is and Who Was and Who Is to Come, the Almighty (the Ruler of all)." AMPC]

94 [Revelation 22:13- "I Am the Alpha and the Omega, the Beginning and the End, the First and the Last." NKJV]

95 [Revelation 19:16- "And He has on His robe and on His thigh a Name written: KING OF KINGS AND LORD OF LORDS." NKJV]

96 [Revelation 5:5- "But one of the elders said to me, 'Do not weep. Behold, the Lion of the Tribe of Judah, the Root of David, has prevailed to open the scroll and to loose its seven seals.'" NKJV]

97 [John 1:29- "Behold! The Lamb of G-d Who takes away the sin of the world." NKJV]

98 [Ephesians 5:2- "And walk in love, as Christ also has loved us and given Himself for us, an offering and a sacrifice to G-d for a sweet-smelling aroma." NKJV]

99 [Colossians 2:14- "having wiped out the handwriting of requirements that was against us, which was contrary to us. And He has taken it out of the way, having nailed it to the cross." NKJV]

100 [Colossians 2:15- "Having disarmed principalities and powers, He made a public spectacle of them, triumphing over them in it." NKJV]

101 [Ephesians 1:20-23- "which He worked in Christ when He raised Him from the dead and seated Him at His right hand in the Heavenly places, far above all principality and power and might and dominion, and every name that is named, not only in this age but also in that which is to come. And He put all things under His feet and gave Him to be Head over all things to the Church, which is His Body, the fullness of Him Who fills all in all." NKJV]

102 [I Peter 1:3, 4- "All praise to G-d, the Father of our LORD Jesus Christ. It is by His great mercy that we have been born again because G-d raised Jesus Christ from the dead. Now we live with great expectation,

and we have a priceless inheritance—an inheritance that is kept in Heaven for you, pure and undefiled, beyond the reach of change and decay." NLT]

103 [I Corinthians 12:27- "Now you are the body of Christ, and members individually." NKJV]

104 [Galatians 2:20- "I have been crucified with Christ; it is no longer I who live, but Christ lives in me; and the life which I now live in the flesh I live by faith in the Son of G-d, who loved me and gave Himself for me." NKJV]

105 [John 14:3b, 4- "I will come again and receive you to Myself; that where I Am, there you may be also. And where I go you know, and the way you know." NKJV]

106 [Matthew 24:36- "But of that day and hour no one knows, not even the angels of Heaven, but My Father Only." NKJV]

107 [John 3:16- "For G-d so loved the world that He gave His Only begotten Son, that whoever believes in Him should not perish but have everlasting life." NKJV; John 5:24- "Most assuredly, I say to you, he who hears My Word and believes in Him Who sent Me has everlasting life, and shall not come into judgment, but has passed from death into Life." NKJV; I John 2:25- "And this is the promise that He has promised us—eternal life." NKJV]

108 [John 14:2, 3- "In My Father's house are many mansions; if it were not so, I would have told you. I go to prepare a place for you. And if I go and prepare a place for you, I will come again and receive you

to Myself; that where I Am, there you may be also." NKJV; Revelation 22:1,2a,3,4- "And he showed me a pure river of water of Life, clear as crystal, proceeding from the throne of G-d and of the Lamb. In the middle of its street, and on either side of the river, was the tree of Life. They shall see His face, and His Name shall be on their foreheads. There shall be no night there: they need no lamp nor light of the sun, for the LORD G-d give them Light. And they shall reign forever and ever." NKJV]

109 [I Corinthians 2:9- "Eye has not seen, nor ear heard, nor have entered into the heart of man the things which G-d has prepared for those who love Him." NKJV]

110 [Revelation 21:4- "He will wipe every tear form their eyes, and there will be no more death or sorrow or crying or pain. All these things are gone forever." NLT]

111 [Revelation 19:7- "Let us be glad and rejoice and let us give honor to Him. For the time has come for the wedding feast of the Lamb, and His bride has prepared herself." NLT]

112 [Revelation 19:8- "She has been permitted to dress in fine (radiant) linen dazzling and white—for the fine linen is (signifies, represents) the righteousness (the upright, just, and godly living, deeds, and conduct, and right standing with G-d) of the saints (G-d's holy people)." AMPC; Ephesians 5:27- "that He might

present her to Himself a glorious church, not having spot or wrinkle or any such thing, but that she should be holy and without blemish." NKJV]

113 [Revelation 19:1- "After these things I heard a loud voice of a great multitude in Heaven, saying, 'Alleluia! Salvation and Glory and Honor and Power belong to the LORD our G-d!' NKJV]

114 [Revelation 21:5, 7- "Then He Who sat on the throne said, 'Behold, I make all things new.' He who overcomes shall inherit all things, and I will be his G-d and he shall be My son." NKJV]

115 [Galatians 6:9- "And let us not grow weary while doing good, for in due season we shall reap if we do not lose heart." NKJV]

116 [Romans 8:38- "For I am persuaded that neither death nor life, nor angels nor principalities nor powers, nor things present nor things to come, not height nor depth, nor any other created thing, shall be able to separate s from the love of G-d which is in Christ Jesus our LORD." NKJV]

117 [I Thessalonians 4:16- "For the LORD Himself will descend from Heaven with a shout, with the voice of an archangel, and with the trumpet of G-d. And the dead in Christ will rise first. The we who are alive and remain shall be caught up together with them in the clouds to meet the LORD in the air. And thus—we shall always be with the LORD." NKJV; Matthew 24:42- "Watch therefore, for you do not know what hour your LORD is coming." NKJV]

My Beloved: A Love Letter

118 [Revelation 22:7- "Behold, I Am coming quickly! Blessed is he who keeps the words of the prophecy of this Book." NKJV]

119 [John 14:16, 17, 26- "And I will pray the Father, and He will give you another Helper, that He may abide with you forever—the Spirit of Truth, Whom the world cannot receive. But the Helper, the Holy Spirit, Whom the Father will and in My Name, He will teach you all things." NKJV]

120 [Ephesians 1:17- "that the G-d of our LORD Jesus Christ, the Father of Glory, may give to you the Spirit of Wisdom and Revelation in the knowledge of Him," NKJV]

121 [John 16:13- "However, when He, the Spirit of Truth, has come, He will guide you into all Truth; for He will not speak on His Own authority, but whatever He hears He will speak; and He will tell you things to come."

122 [Colossians 1:25b, 26- "to make the Word of G-d fully know (among you)—the mystery of which was hidden for ages and generations (from angels and men) but is now revealed to His holy people (the saints)." AMPC]

123 [Titus 2:13- "Looking for the Blessed Hope and Glorious appearing of our great G-d and Savior Jesus Christ." NKJV]

124 [Isaiah 43:4- "Since you were precious in My sight, you have been honored, and I have loved you." NKJV; Ephesians 2:4- "But, G- is so rich in mercy, and He

loved us so much, that even though we were dead because of our sins, He gave us Life when He raised Christ from the dead. (It is only by G-d's grace that you have been saved! For He raised us from the dead along with Christ and seated us with Him in the Heavenly realms because we are united with Christ Jesus." NLT]

125 [I John 4:19- "We love Him, because He first loved us." AMPC]

126 [Matthew 11:28- "Then Jesus said, 'Come to Me, all of you who are weary and carry heavy burdens, and I will give you rest." NLT]

127 [Psalms 91:1- "He that dwelleth in the secret place of the Most High shall abide under the shadow of the Almighty." KJV]

128 [John 4:10- "Jesus answered and said to her, 'If you knew the Gift of G-d, and Who it Is Who says to you, 'Give Me a drink', you would have asked Him, and He would have given you Living Water." NKJV]

129 [Revelation 21:6- "I am the Alpha and Omega, the beginning, and the end. I will give of the fountain of the water of life freely to him who thirsts." NKJV]

130 [John 7:38- "Anyone who believes in Me may come and drink! For the Scriptures declare, 'Rivers of Living Water will flow from His heart.'" NLT]

131 [Luke 10:2- "He said to them, 'The harvest truly is great, but the laborers are few; therefore, pray the LORD of the Harvest to send out laborers into His Harvest.'" NKJV]

132 [Psalms 42:1- "As the deer pants for the water brooks, so pants my soul for You, O G-d." NKJV]

133 [Revelation 19:7- "For the time has come for the Wedding Feast of the Lamb, and His bride has prepared herself." NLT]

134 [Song of Solomon 2:16- "My Beloved is mine, and I am His." NKJV]

135 [Song of Solomon 2:10-12- "My Beloved spoke, and said to me: 'Rise up, My Love, My fair one, and come away. For lo, the winter is past, the rain is over and gone. The flowers appear on the earth; the time of singing has come." NKJV]

136 [Song of Solomon 8:6, 7- "Set Me as a seal upon your heart, as a seal upon your arm. Many waters cannot quench love, nor can the floods drown it." NKJV]

Made in the USA
Columbia, SC
29 March 2024